YOUR KNOWLEDGE HAS VALUE

Bibliographic information published by the German National Library:

The German National Library lists this publication in the National Bibliography; detailed bibliographic data are available on the Internet at http://dnb.dnb.de .

Imprint:

Copyright © 2015 GRIN Verlag, Open Publishing GmbH
Print and binding: Books on Demand GmbH, Norderstedt Germany
ISBN: 9783656986836

This book at GRIN:

http://www.grin.com/en/e-book/336980/insurance-steering-in-the-irish-motor-trade-industry

Lindsay Pulsford

Insurance Steering in the Irish Motor Trade Industry

GRIN Publishing

GRIN - Your knowledge has value

Since its foundation in 1998, GRIN has specialized in publishing academic texts by students, college teachers and other academics as e-book and printed book. The website www.grin.com is an ideal platform for presenting term papers, final papers, scientific essays, dissertations and specialist books.

Visit us on the internet:

http://www.grin.com/

http://www.facebook.com/grincom

http://www.twitter.com/grin_com

Contents

1. Introduction

This paper hopes to give a closer examination and overview of an issue which is ever prominent, but often overlooked. Insurance Steering in the Motor Trade Industry is the practice by where insurers pressure, mislead and forcefully imply to consumers that they must use one of their "approved" or "preferred" repairers. While this practice benefits the insurance company, and often even the consumer due to financial incentives to take the insurers advice, it has led to many body-shops across the country being excluded. Any bodyshop not in this exclusive network of repairers have found themselves in a rather precarious position. While complaints have been made that this is anti-competitive and harming the market, as well as consumer welfare and choice, the claims have failed to be heard in Ireland.

Looking towards other jurisdictions both America and the UK have found themselves dealing with similar issues. The American perspective shows us where case law could potentially take us years down the line, as anti-steering legislation has already been enacted in some states. While the UK can show us how to deal with those first few stages of handling the issue, as is happening currently there.

This paper will aim to:

- Demonstrate how this practice is potentially anti-competitive

- Refer to relevant Irish, European and American sources

- Evaluate the current state of the market, particularly by utilising Irish primary sources (questionnaires and email correspondence)

- Assess the Insurance Law aspect

- Assess the Competition Law aspect

- Determine the role the consumer, and consumer welfare has in all of this

2. Insurance Law in Ireland

In Ireland activities of non-life insurance have been regulated since the 1930's. Back as far as the Insurance Act 1936 reference is made to the "mechanically propelled vehicle insurance business" which recognised the need for insurance against loss or damage to, or arising out

2

of, or in connection with the use of these vehicles, including third party risks.[1] Similarly a parallel term for motor vehicle insurance including "all liability arising out of the use of motor vehicles operating on the land (including carrier's liability)" can be found at a European level.[2]

The obligation to insure has also been placed in a motor vehicle-specific light as it is listed as an obligation under the Road Traffic Act.[3] Provisions in relation to obligations of both the insurer and an insured in respect of the approved policy are laid out,[4] and said insurance is to be "against all sums without limit".[5]

Further Statutory developments in the area include the Insurance Act 1989, the Insurance Act 2000,[6] and the Non-Life Insurance (Provision of Information) (Renewal of Policy of Insurance) Regulations 2007.[7] The two former acts contain little mention of non-life insurance, and no mention specific to motor insurance. The latter however contains useful definitions of terminology relevant to the area: "insurance"[8], "motor insurance"[9], "private motor insurance"[10] and "term"[11]. Following this the main thoughts of the Regulations pertain to the ability of the Minister to require information and the rules for policy renewals.

The insurance industry is regulated by the Central Bank of Ireland.[12] Under the Insurance Act 1989 the Central Bank has extensive powers covering all aspects of the insurance industry. It

---

[1] Insurance Act 1936, section 3.

[2] European Communities (Non-Life Insurance) Regulations (1994) Schedule 1 (A)(10).

[3] Road Traffic Act 1961, section 56.

[4] Road Traffic Act 1961, section 62.

[5] Road Traffic Act 1961, section 56(1)(a).

[6] The Insurance Act of 2000 contains amendments of the 1989 Act, the 1936 Act, the 1995 Act and the Central Bank Act 1989.

[7] Non-Life Insurance (Provision of Information) (Renewal of Policy of Insurance) Regulations (2007), S.I. No. 74/2007.

[8] An insurance of one or more of classes 1, 2, 3, 7, 8, 9, 10 and 13 specified in Part A of Annex I to the European Communities (Non-Life Insurance) Framework Regulations 1994 (S.I. 359 of 1994).

[9] Means insurance of classes 3 (excluding land vehicles other than motor vehicles), and 10 (excluding carrier's liability) as specified in Part A of Annex I to the European Communities (Non-Life Insurance) Framework Regulations of 1994.

[10] "A policy of motor insurance taken out by an individual alone or with another person, outside of that individual's business, trade or profession."

[11] "The risks to be covered in the policy of motor insurance, the restrictions, if any, that are different, in the policy of motor insurance that is to be renewed, to those that apply to the policy of motor insurance that is in operation, any change to the policy of motor insurance, and the premium for the policy of motor insurance to be renewed."

[12] Dillon Eustace, A Guide to Non-Life Regulation in Ireland (February 2011) <http://hb.betterregulation.com/external/A%20Guide%20to%20Non-Life%20Insurance%20Regulation%20in%20Ireland.pdf> (visited 17 December 2014).

is the competent authority for the authorisation and ongoing supervision of insurers.[13] Insurers must also comply with certain conditions[14]: there must be a 'class 10 undertaking', within the meaning of regulation 2(1) of the 1976 EU Regulations. The undertaking must be carrying out non-life insurance in the State, from an establishment in the State with the correct authorisation to do so, or the undertaking must be for the purposes of carrying non-life insurance by way of services into the State from an establishment in another Member State[15]. In addition to this the insurer must be a member of MIBI.[16]

Utmost good faith is a principle characteristic of the insurance contract.[17] It is a contract *uberrimae fidei*, based upon exercise of good faith by each party involved.[18] The duty to disclose all relevant material facts is inherent in the nature of the insurance contract and any inequalities of knowledge on part of any party ought to be rectified as much, and as soon as possible.[19] Often, a "co-operations clause" will be found in insurance policies requiring the insured to, for example, provide details of the loss, for the undertaking not to take any steps prejudicing the insurer's position or for the undertaking not to settle with a third party.[20] For example with motor insurance the insured is not obligated to admit liability to a third party. A breach of the insured's duty to co-operate will defeat the claim. In the UK it has been held that prejudice is not a factor which has been taken into account when considering whether a claims co-operation clause has been breached.[21]

There have been suggestions in the past that the insurance industry deserves an immunity from competition law.[22] The Oireachtas rejected this, and there is no exception in the Competition Acts for any industry[23]. In a case mirroring the issues arising in the motor trade industry, the Competition Authority refused to certify or license a notified agreement where a travel agency compelled its customers to purchase their travel insurance from a particular

---

[13] <http://www.centralbank.ie/regulation/industry-sectors/insurance-companies/non-life-insurance-companies/Pages/default.aspx> (visited 18 December 2014).

[14] Attracta O'Regan Cazabon, *Insurance Law in Ireland* (Round Hall Sweet and Maxwell, 1999) at 172, at [12.40].

[15] Robert Pierse, *Road Traffic Law* (2nd ed., Butterworths, 1995) at 548, at [8.5].

[16] Motor Insurer's Bureau of Ireland.

[17] O'Regan Cazabon, note 14, at 44, at [3.01].

[18] Doyle J in *Inspector Murphy v PMPA Insurance Company* [1978] I.L.R.M 29.

[19] Foster B in *Abbot v Howard* (1832) Hayes 381 at 423.

[20] John Lowry, Philip Rawlings and Robert Merkin, *Insurance Law: Doctrines and Principles* (3rd ed., Hart Publishing, 2011) at 306.

[21] *Shinedean Ltd. v Alldown Demolition (London) Ltd.* [2006] EWCA Civ 939.

[22] Rolf Nebel, "Application of Competition Law in the Insurance Industry" [1993] 5 ECLR 189.

[23] Vincent Power, *Competition Law and Practice* (Tottel, 2007) at 1246.

broker[24]. The Authority objected to this and the arrangement was changed so that using this particular insurer was merely an option for customers. Seeing as this tying agreement was not allowed it is presumable the similar practice in the motor trade industry could be viewed in the same way. This, teamed with the added pressure placed on consumers, a degree of undue influence and offerings of financial incentives, all have a cumulative effect of making this a major issue in the industry.

2.a. The Claims Process

Following a traffic accident there are a number of steps to be taken when making a claim. The National Claims Assessment Service provides information in layman's terms as to what to do directly following an accident, but little as to how to deal with the insurance companies themselves.[25] While individual insurance companies have individual procedures in place, it is important for the average policy holder to understand the process from an unbiased perspective. Consumer websites can help with this, www.consumerhelp.ie provides a basic guide as to what to do when making a claim[26]. Proper claims procedure is outlined under the Consumer Protection Code 2012.[27]

Often after a car accident, the (future) claimant will find themselves in an unfamiliar situation. Making a claim with your insurance company is not a task one undertakes on a daily basis. It is presumable that the party involved will be unsure of their situation. While certain research can be done on a personal level, people place their faith in their insurance company, comfortable in the knowledge that they know what is best. In this near state of vulnerability one could find themselves susceptible to the wills of their insurance company. As once stated "Insurance itself is not a problem. Suffering a loss without adequate protection is a problem. Insurance is part of the solution, but most people are more afraid of the solution than they are of the problem".[28] People desire for this situation to dematerialise as speedily as possible and thus are more than willing to go along with whatever they are told. This could have less than favourable consequences as insurance companies find themselves at a significant advantage, they have the knowledge and the power in this set up. In this flurry of

---

[24] Dec No 274, *Falcon Holidays/Ben McArdle Ltd*, 4 Feb 1994 and Notif CA/31/92E.
[25] <http://www.claim.ie/Road_Accident> (visited 20 December 2014).
[26] <http://www.consumerhelp.ie/making-a-claim> (visited 20 December 2014).
[27] Consumer Protection Code 2012, section 7.6 to 7.21.
[28] Brian H. Breuel, *The Complete Idiots Guide to Buying Insurance and Annuities* (Alpha, 1996).

claims and insurance jargon there is a tangible risk of basic consumer rights being abused. The Consumer Protection Code outlines these fundamentals, sections of particular relevance include that regulated entities:

- Do not recklessly, negligently or deliberately mislead a customer as to the real or perceived advantages or disadvantages of any product or service[29]

- Do not exert undue pressure or undue influence on a customer[30]

- Act honestly, fairly and professionally in the best interests of its customers and the integrity of the market[31]

- Act with due skill, care and diligence in the best interests of its customers[32]

This paper seeks to explore whether these general principles have been complied with. While insurance steering undoubtedly restricts consumer choice, is it at play in the motor insurance industry? Are the requests of insurance companies for consumers to use "approved" repairers made in utmost good faith and merely suggestions, or is there a more pressurised element to it, and is this in turn an anti-competitive practice?

3. Competition Act 2002

The Irish Competition Act 2002 states in Section 4 that all agreements between undertakings which have as their object or effect the prevention, distortion or restriction of competition are prohibited.[33] There is some ambiguity as to the actual meaning of this. "Prevention", "distortion" and "restriction" are not defined in the Act. The Irish courts have generally favoured a "rule of reason" approach. It has been stated that if this provision is to be literally interpreted, virtually every form of business agreement could be said to be a violation[34]. The Irish view, when assessing a potential breach of Section 4(1) is that the key consideration is definition of the relevant market[35]. Under s4(2) an arrangement in breach of s4(1) may not be

---

[29] Ibid, section 2.3.
[30] Ibid, section 2.9.
[31] Ibid, section 2.1.
[32] Ibid, section 2.2.
[33] Competition Act 2002, section 4(1).
[34] Dec No 1, *Nallen/O'Toole* 2 April 1992, Notif CA/8/91.
[35] Alan WJ McCarthy and Vincent Power, *Irish Competition Law: The Competition Act 2002* (Tottel, 2006) at 54.

prohibited if it meets the efficiency conditions set out under s4(5). There are four conditions and the conditions in question must meet all four cumulatively:

1. Must contribute to improving the production or distribution of goods or services or to promoting technical or economic progress

2. While allowing consumers a fair share of the benefit

3. Does not impose on undertakings concerned terms which are not indispensable to the attainment of those objectives

4. Does not afford undertakings the possibility of eliminating competition in respect of a substantial part of the products or services in question

It is a safe assumption that insurance companies would attempt to have their preferred repairer arrangements come under these four conditions. It could be said that distribution of the service is improved through a more efficient channel, that consumers receive benefit from this and that all autobody repairers have the opportunity to enter a preferred repairer arrangement with them, thus not eliminating a substantial part of the market. While these may be valid arguments, the opposite could also be argued, that there is a hampering to the distribution of this service as full choice and disclosure is not being afforded, that consumers welfare is being damaged by this and that actually obtaining an arrangement of this kind with a large insurance company is simply not a realistic feat for a small bodyshop, thus leaving them closed off to the market.

4. The Place of the Consumer in Competition Law

4.a. The Rights of the Consumer, a Competition Law Objective?

EU opinion of the objective of competition law has evolved over time. In 1966 the conclusion was drawn that EU Competition law had the goal of achieving single/common market integration.[36] This later developed into protecting the participants of the competitive process and effective competition.[37] More recently the European Commission has put forward the idea that the leading objective is consumer welfare. In the case of *GlaxoSmithKline* it was

---

[36] *Établissements Consten S.à.R.L. and Grundig-Verkaufs-GmbH v Commission of the European Economic Community* (56/64, 58/64) [1966] E.C.R. 299 at 340.
[37] European Commission, XV Annual Report on Competition Policy 1985 (1986).

argued that anything decreasing consumer welfare qualifies as anti-competitive conduct.[38] While the General Court and the EU Commission agreed with this the Court of Justice did not, claiming that consumer protection is part of the structure of competition law, and it is this structure that EU competition policy has the goal of protecting.[39] This is supported by Articles 101 and 102 of the TFEU, which are more concerned with the protection of the competition in markets, rather than consumer welfare. This being said, consumer welfare is an integral part of the competition structure. If competition in the markets is fair, improved welfare for consumers is a presumable knock-on effect from this.

The role of competition law is to oversee the whole competitive process, consisting of:

- Competitors

    o The supply side.

- Competitive Environment

    o No boundaries or unnecessary restriction on competition (including restrictive agreements)

- Market

    o Different markets being suitable to different forms of competition due to differing product natures, consumer choices, *etc.*

- Consumers

    o The demand side

- Product (or service) plus substitutes[40]

Under this structure consumers and their welfare are not the ultimate aim of competition policy, but rather one of a few. One of the factors here cannot flourish without the other. They are all responsive elements, whose interplay and successful functioning result in satisfactory protection of competition policy, which is the main objective to be attained here.

---

[38] *GlaxoSmithKline v Commission (T-168/01)* [2006] E.C.R. II-2969 at [171]-[172].

[39] Can be found in the GlaxoSmithKline appeal: *GlaxoSmithKline Services Unlimited v Commission of the EC (C-501/06 P, C-513/06 P, C-515/06 P, C-519/06 P)* [2009] 4 C.M.L.R. 2 at [63].

[40] Barbora Jedličková, "One among many or one above all? The role of consumers and their welfare in competition law and policy" (2012), 33(12) ECLR 574.

4.b. The Role of Competition Authorities

The EU has broad powers when it comes to competition law, the ability to extensively investigate[41] and place heavy fines on undertakings for wrongdoings.[42] The €1 billion fine placed on Intel for abuse of dominant position demonstrates just how significant the EU has become in this field of law.[43] However in 2003 National Competition Authorities were given the power to enforce EU competition law, thus creating a network throughout the Union.[44] While response to this has generally been favourable, it is inevitable that there will be clashes between national and EU law on some issue at some point.

In March 2012, the UK decided to abolish the Office of Fair Trading (OFT) and the Competition Commission (CC) and combine together to form a single Competition and Market Authority (CMA). The CMA ultimately will separate the strands of consumer protection law and competition law. The CC has recognised that the role of a competition authority should be to protect competition through means of increasing welfare, productivity, economic growth and innovation, with a link to consumer protection, as competition benefits the consumer.[45] However the OFT has expressed concerns that the division could potentially be harmful, as consumer protection law and competition law are so intrinsically linked it could be imperative to separate the strands.[46] While both organisations agree consumer protection plays a major role in competition law the OFT sees it as the primary goal, while the CC sees it as one of many. The CC is of the belief that through promotion of competition law, consumer protection will follow, while the OFT believes that they should be implemented side-by-side.

In July 2014 the Competition and Consumer Protection Act was enacted in Ireland.[47] Amongst other matters, this Act merged the Competition Authority with the National

---

[41] See Ch. V and VI, Council Regulation 1/2003 of 16 December 2002 on the Implementation of the Rules on Competition laid down in Articles 81 and 82 of the Treaty [2003] OJ L1/1.

[42] EC Commission, "Guidelines on the method of Setting Fines" pursuant to Article 23(2)(a) of Regulation No 1/2003 [2006] OJ C210/2.

[43] Memo of the European Commission, Antitrust: Commission welcomes General Court judgment Upholding its Decision Against Intel, (2014) MEMO/14/416.

[44] Imelda Maher, "A Fine Balance, The National Courts, The European Commission and EU Competition Law" (2011) 1 DULJ 153.

[45] Competition Commission, "Competition Consultation", p.20; *Competition Commission, "Empowering and Protecting Consumers: Consultation on Institutional Changes for Provision of Consumer Information, Education, Advocacy, and Enforcement: Competition Commission Response"* (September 2011), at 2.

[46] OFT, "A Competition Regime for Growth: A Consultation on Options for Reform, The OFT's Response to the Government's Consultation" (June 2011) (OFT, Competition Consultation), at 5, [1.6].

[47] The Competition and Consumer Protection Act entered into force on the 31st October 2014.

Consumer Agency.[48] This is a move that would seem to suggest the Irish Authorities see consumer protection as on par with competition policy, rather than a mere, albeit important, factor of the process. The new body is called the Competition and Consumer Protection Commission,[49] a name which supports the suggestion that great significance is placed on the Consumer Protection role, self-described as a "dual mandate".[50]

5. The Competition Authority in Ireland

In 2012 the Central Bank published the Consumer Protection Code, which stated the entities were to act fairly, honestly and professionally in the best interests of consumers and the interests of the market.[51] On foot of this (as well as a number of complaints and some political attention on the area[52]), the Competition Authority decided to take a long overdue look at the possibility of anti-competitive behaviour in the insurance industry.

In their *Guidance Note on Preferred Repairer Arrangements in the Insurance Sector,*[53] through very selective and often flawed reasoning, the Competition Authority comes to the conclusion that there is no infringement of Section 4 of the 2002 Act[54] and /or Article 101 TFEU.[55] The report focuses on arrangements in the motor vehicle and home insurance sectors, however it is the former which is the main subject. Throughout, the phrase "competition law and policy is to protect competition, not to protect firms that are having trouble competing"[56] becomes somewhat of a mantra for the Competition Authority and is the sole basis behind most of its reasoning.

The benefits of preferred repairer arrangements are highlighted from the outset, it is submitted that the strong financial incentives, speed and efficiency all make these arrangements sound and worthwhile. Insurers are now more actively involved in claims

---

[48] The Competition and Consumer Protection Act 2014, Chapter 3. Also the Act repeals part 4 of the Competition Act 2002, and part 2 of the Consumer Act 2007.

[49] Sheila Tormey, "Legislative Comment- Ireland: the Competition and Consumer Protection Act 2014" (2014) 35 ECLR 534.

[50] <http://www.ccpc.ie/who-we-are> (visited 29 December 2014).

[51] Consumer Protection Code 2012, General Principles, s2.1.

[52] See Robert Dowds Speech, "Government Action is needed to End Insurance Company 'Steering'" (November 2011).

[53] Competition Authority Guidance Note: Preferred Repairer Arrangements in the Insurance Sector (December 2012).

[54] Competition Act 2002, section 4.

[55] Treaty for the Functioning of the European Union, Article 101.

[56] CA Guidance Note, note 53, Executive Summary, page 1.

management. "Claims are the largest costs that insurers face"[57], and these arrangements help lower and manage these costs for insurance companies. Given that the function of an insurance company is to pay out claims for its paying policy holders, the phrasing of this comment and tone suggest that it is somewhat of a burden on insurance companies and that they should be entitled to attempt to lower their expenditure in this area at all costs. One cannot help but see this as a somewhat flawed argument- seeking to minimise costs is one matter, whereas walking the line between competitive and anti-competitive behaviour is another.

It is said that effective claims costs management should benefit policyholders through lower premiums. "Should" is the optimum word here. While on paper this looks promising, in practice this would not foreseeably happen. The insurance industry is one with some oligopolistic features, if one insurer significantly lowers its premiums, others will presumably, follow suit. It is difficult to determine whether these "savings" would be passed on to policyholders or merely retained as profit. The *Guidance Note* provides no substantive evidence that this practice, which has been happening for a number of years now, has in fact benefited consumers in any way and relies upon vague auxiliary verbs to convey its point.

When assessing the exclusivity of preferred repairer arrangements the concept of anti-competitive foreclosure arises. On the surface, by pure definition standard it fits the situation at hand, firms being unable to access a significant proportion of the market due to the effect of an agreement or network of agreements.[58] The *Guidance Note* finds that no evidence that these arrangements are exclusive and that even the cumulative effect of these arrangements would not be significant to a closing off of the market and potential elimination of competition for some. It is argued that consumers still have freedom of choice and that the preferred repairers are merely suggestions, however this is far from the case. It is a lack of information here that causes the problem. Consumers, suffering a car accident, find themselves in a vulnerable position, one they presumably are not in too often. Many people have a lack of understanding as to how the process of making a claim works and are susceptible to believing what their insurance company tells them, so when they are coerced and influenced into choosing a particular repairer, offered incentives to choose said repairer and not informed of the option of using their own local mechanic, it has the overall effect of hampering their freedom of choice. Although there is no outright obligation to use the

---

[57] Ibid, at 5, [2.13].
[58] Ibid, at 9 [3.16].

preferred repairer on the consumer's part it is implied that the obligation remains. To take a basic example a person making a purchase in a shop has a choice between product A and product B, however the seller only informs them of the availability of A and neglects to mention the potential availability of B. Theoretically there is still a choice on the customers part, but it unfairly influenced the external factors which place pressure on him to decide a certain way. This is similar to the process of selecting an autobody repairer following an accident, one finds themselves under the impression that one option (namely, the right to choose your own repairer) is unavailable, or not feasible from the insurer's point of view. While an insurer may argue that the choice was always there, the lack of information pertaining to it means that in reality, its presence, or lack-there-off was redundant. While it can be claimed that consumers are capable of making the necessary informed decision of this matter to their own account, the fact remains that this is a complex area. This means there is a tangible risk that certain consumers are left exposed in a market where expectations of self-awareness are pitched too highly.[59]

One final point of critical analysis on this *Guidance Note* are the examples from other jurisdictions presented, particularly the example of the USA. It is cited that in the United States arrangements of this type are not seen as anti-competitive, with case law of *Proctor v State Farm*[60] and *Quality v Allstate*[61] provided to back up the claim. What the Authority has failed to note here is that these cases are more than 30 years old, from 1982 and 1981 respectively. The former case was a ruling from a District Court for the District of Columbia, and the latter a case from the 7th Circuit Court of Appeals, based in Illinois, acting as an appellate for Illinois, Indiana and Wisconsin.[62] These states were, mostly likely purposefully picked as examples as they are not part of the 35 American States which have anti-steering issues in their legislation.[63] A false view is given by this *Guidance Note* that all American jurisdictions find insurance steering to be a fine practice, when in fact roughly 70% have found the opposite. There has also been an abundance of case law in the last 30 years which would have better illustrated the general stance on preferred repairer arrangements in the USA. The fact that the Authority had to bring up case law from three decades ago to prove its point does a lot to illustrate the strength of its argument.

---

[59] Stephen Weatherill, *EU Consumer Law and Policy* (Edward Elgar, 2005) at 113.
[60] *Phillip M. Proctor v. State Farm Mutual Automobile Insurance Company* 675 F.2d 308 (D.C. Cir. 1982).
[61] *Quality Auto Body Inc v Allstate Insurance Company* 660 F2d 1195 (1981).
[62] Wisconsin is one of the 35 states which has anti-steering policies in its legislation. See Chapter 632 of Wisconsin State Legislature, Subchapter IV, Automobile and Motor Vehicle Insurance, [632.37].
[63] <http://www.stopdrp.com/steering-laws-by-state.html> (visited October 2nd 2014).

While the *Guidance Note* is a helpful tool in assessing these alleged insurance industry practices it is clear to see they have been selective in what they have included, and not included. It is recommendable that a more thorough report be assembled. One that properly assesses the potential anti-competitive foreclosure issue, uses case law from the last decade and realises that while competition law is not about protecting the competitor having trouble competing, but that overtly shutting them off from the market is not only damaging to them, but also to the consumers interest.

Previous to this the Competition Authority released a report and recommendations for the non-life insurance market as a whole[64]. While it was recognised that there is not much rivalry in the motor insurance industry there still is a need to lower the entry barriers to the market.[65] The report is more focused on issues of price transparency with quotes, uninsured drivers, reductions in legal created boundaries and the position of intermediaries. There is no mention of insurance steering per se, however, it is stated that these recommendations are designed so to facilitate informed decision making on the part of consumers[66]. This is a common goal shared with the objective of anti-steering rule. It is not a desire to cause damage to insurance business or raise costs, but rather allow for more independent, knowledgeable judgment in this area.

6. A European Stance

As mentioned above Articles of the TFEU are the driving force behind EU competition law, particularly Art 101, which is the principle vehicle for the control of anti-competitive agreements. The extent to which economic analysis should and actually does occur within the bounds of Article 101(1) and the interpretation of Art 101(3), including whether non-economic factors should be taken into consideration is a point of much discussion. The answer to these questions has evolved accordingly over time with case law.

The ultimate objective of competition law is enhancing efficiency – achieving optimal allocation of resources while achieving maximum consumer welfare. Looking towards

---

[64] The Competition Authority, Competition Issues in the Non-Life Insurance Market (March 2005).
[65] Ibid. at 4-5.
[66] Ibid. at 5.

tradition economic theory, the general suggestion is that where there is workable competition, goods and services will be produced more efficiently.[67]

Art 101(1) states that all agreements, decision and concerted practices between undertakings[68] having as their object of effect the prevention, restriction or distortion of competition shall be prohibited. There is an issue that arises here. In many situations an agreement may have featured which both enhance and restrict competition. It is proposed that EU competition law should adopt a stance of weighing the pros and cons of the agreement in question, in effect, balancing the anti-competitive effects against the pro-competitive ones. A stance like this could be of benefit to the motor insurance industry, as it would be necessary to balance the effects of insurance steering and assess the competitiveness of the practice (for example: the benefits of convenience to customers versus the restriction of choice, the perks of being an "approved repairer" versus potentially closing others off from the market).

One argument is that the EU should follow the stance taken in the United States. Section 1 of the Sherman Act[69] states that every contract, conspiracy or combination the restrains trade is illegal. This was later clarified in that only undue or unreasonable restraints should be condemned.[70] Basically a distinction is made between a rule of reason and *per se* rules. The decision of whether an agreement promotes or supresses competition will lie on a balancing of the pro- and anti-competitive effects of said agreement.[71] The argument is affected by Art 101(3), whereby the agreement contributes to improving production or distribution of goods and/or promoting technical or economic progress, whilst allowing consumers a fair share of the benefit. No provision of this kind exists in the US, validating the need for rule of reason. It is submitted that, seeing as the EU already has Art 101(3) the need for a rule of reason is obsolete. Other arguments against the introduction of the rule of reason claim that the introduction could lead to confusion and misleading comparisons with U.S. anti-trust law.[72] However the counter stance would be that the Commission are far too formalistic and narrow-minded in their approach, and if national courts were to follow this practice,

---

[67] Fredric Scherer and David Ross, *Industrial Market Structure and Economic Performance* (3rd ed., Houghton Mifflin, 1990).

[68] "Undertaking" meaning any entity engaged in economic activity regardless of methods of financing or legal status. Case C-41/90 *Hofner and Elser v Macroton GmbH* [1991] ECR I-1979.

[69] The Sherman Act 1890.

[70] *Standard Oil v US* 221 U.S. (1911) as per White CJ.

[71] *National Society of Professional Engineers v US*, 435, US 679, 691-692 (1978).

[72] Richard Whish and Brenda Surfin, "Article 85 and the Rule of Reason" (1987) 7 YBEL 12-20, at 36.

agreements which could be beneficial, and actually increase competition, are not being made.[73]

In its *Guidelines on Art 101(3)*[74] the potential for positive economic effects are recognised.[75]Certain efficiencies flowing from these particular agreement, may redeem said agreement, in that they create additional value, lower costs or improve the product offered.[76] This could potentially be an argument to the favour of the insurance companies as the practice of insurance steering might come under Art101(1), but could be considered to have the pro-competitive effects outweigh the negative ones under the Art 101(3) exceptions.

When it comes to case law regarding article 101 a distinction needs to be ascertained as to whether it is the "object" or the "effect" which is anti-competitive in nature. Should the "object" of the agreement be anti-competitive, or have the potential to have a negative impact on competition[77] it will immediately come under Art 101(1), however in all other circumstances (i.e. when it is not plainly clear the agreement is a violation) economic context as well as the formal terms must be taken into consideration in order to assess the potential effect it could have on the market.[78] This principle was brought to the fore in the *STM* case[79] where it was accepted that the words of Art 101 were to be taken in a disjunctive way, certain forms of collusion by undertakings are condemning right to their very core, and thus need no further pressing.[80] Proof of existence of such agreement will suffice.[81] It is unnecessary to demonstrate any actual effects or the parties' intentions.

Should the anti-competitiveness of an agreement not transpire when looking to the objective, it is needed to move to consideration of the effects.[82] Account is to be taken as to the actual conditions in which the agreement functions unless the agreement contains obvious restrictions such as price-fixing, market-sharing or control of outlets,[83] these restrictions can only be weighed against their pro-competitive effects in the context of Art 101(3) and would

---

[73] Valentine Korah, "The Rise and Fall of Provisional Validity – The Need for a Rule of Reason in EEC Antitrust" (1981) 3 North Western Journal of International Business Law, 320, at 354.
[74] Guidelines I the application of Article [101(3)] of the Treaty Guidelines OJ [2004] C 130/1
[75] Ibid. at [32].
[76] Ibid. at [33], with [51] outlining that they must be substantially verified.
[77] Case C-8/08 *T-Mobile Netherlands* [2009] ECR I-4529.
[78] Richard Whish and David Bailey, *Competition Law* (7th ed., Oxford University Press, 2012) at 630.
[79] Case 56/65 *Societe La Technique Minere v Maschinenbau Ulm GmbH* [1996] ECR 235.
[80] Okeoghene Odudu, "Interpreting Article 81(1): Object as Subjective Intention" (2001) 26 EL Rev 60.
[81] Commission Guidelines on the Application of Article 81(3) [2004] OJ C101/97 [21]-[23].
[82] Case C-234/89 *Delimitis v Henninger Brau AG* [1991] ECR I-935.
[83] Cases T- 374/94 *European Night Services v Commission* [1998] ECR II-3141, [1998] 5 CMLR 718, para 136.

be considered to go to the object of the agreement. The condition that a restriction be necessary leads to a two-fold examination. First it must be established whether the restriction is objectively necessary for the implementation of the main operation and second, whether it is proportionate.[84]

In the *Crehan*[85] judgement the relationship of Art 101(1) and 101(3) addressed as well as the often tumultuous relationship between national and EU courts. The case concerned tied-house agreements, by which a pub agrees with a brewery to only serve their products. Despite the pub tenant being in a significantly weaker position from a negotiation standpoint due to the brewery's extensive network of agreements, the English Courts overturned a decision stating that this was anti-competitive and foreclosing the market.[86] The European Commission stated that while these agreements did come under Art 101(1) they qualified for exemption under Art 101(3) (then Art 81(1) and 81(3) respectively). In the High Court an extensive examination was executed and rejected the Commission's findings of foreclosure, however this was overturned by the Court of Appeal where it was stated the High Court should have never gone into such detailed factual analysis of the area and should not have "second guessed" the Commission's findings.[87]

7. Assessing the Market

The motor insurance market is one that contains certain oligopolistic qualities. The market structure in place is one dominated by a few large producers of similar products. In 2003, the four leading motor insurers accounted for 70% of the premiums on the market.[88] They engage in strategic behaviour which acts in their own self-interest while taking into account the behaviour of others in the market.[89] It is a situation of mutual interdependence. Oligopolistic interdependence must not be overstated however. These market structures are rarely

---

[84] Case T 112/99 *Metropole Television (M6) Suez-Lyonnaise des Eaux, France Telecom, and Television Francaise 1 SA (TF1) v Commission* [2001] ECR II-2459, [106].
[85] C-435/99 *Courage Ltd v Crehan* [1999] ECR I-6297.
[86] *Crehan v Inntrepreneur CPC* [2003] EWHC 1510, Reversed in Appeal in *Crehan v Inntrepreneur CPC* [2004] EWCa Civ 637.
[87] Maher, note 44.
[88] CA paper 2005, see note 64.
[89] Stanley Brue, Campbell McConnell and Sean Flynn, *Essentials of Economics* (3rd ed., McGraw Hill Irwin, 2014) at 211.

symmetrical, with identical goods at similar costs. The reality is far more complex than that.[90] In addition to this there are also barriers to entry, with large economies of scale at play. It is this dominance which allows insurance companies to found "preferred repairer" arrangements. By doing which they enable themselves to lower costs and be more competitive themselves.

7.a. Anti- Competitive Foreclosure

Foreclosure is a means by stopping firms from entering a market or preventing existing competitors from growing within it. In assessing the motor insurance industry and "preferred repairer" agreements, this definition certainly seems like a correct fit. However it is necessary to determine whether this practice amounts to anti-competitive foreclosure or mere foreclosure.

Before this, it must be recognised that foreclosure may be horizontal or vertical. The former is where the dominant firm takes action to exclude a competitor from supplying, while the latter is when a dominant firm takes action to exclude a competitor in the downstream market[91].

Fig. 2.1 **Horizontal Foreclosure**

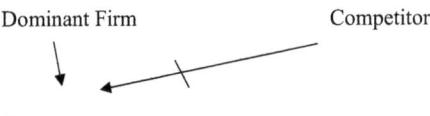

Fig 2.2 **Vertical Foreclosure**

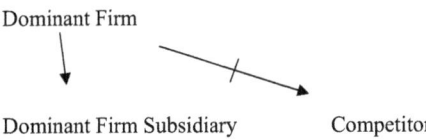

---

[90] Paul Craig and Grainne DeBurca, *European Law: Text, Cases and Materials* (5th ed., Oxford University Press, 2011), at 966.

[91] Whish and Bailey, note 78, at 204-205 (including Fig. 5.1 and Fig 5.2).

While the insurer/repairer relationship is not that of a dominant firm in the marketplace (at least not in the sense of Art 102 TFEU) the similarities of this complex situation are ignorable. Insurance companies, through their arrangements, are effectively closing off the market to certain repairers. The issues currently arising in this market mimic foreclosure and exclusionary practices which are deemed unfair competition by many EU writings. In the *Guidelines on Art 102 Enforcement Priorities* it is stated that the aim of its enforcement activity in relation to exclusionary abused is to ensure that the dominant undertakings do not impair effective competition by foreclosing their competitors in an anti-competitive way.[92] This would be different than mere foreclosure, where a dominant undertaking wins business on the merits as result of superior efficiency.[93] The Commission has laid out factors for determining whether anti-competitive conduct is present:[94]

- Position of the dominant undertaking in the market.

Seeing as the insurer/repairer industries are more complementary of one another this is difficult to determine. However, it is the insurance company which operates on a higher scale, thus making it the dominant one of the two.

- Conditions on the relevant market.

Including conditions of entry and expansion, economies of scale.

- Position of dominant undertaking's competitors

- Position of customers or input suppliers.

Which includes possible selectivity of the conduct in question. This may include the dominant undertaking applying a practice to selected input suppliers who are of particular importance for the entry or expansion of competitors.

- Extent of allegedly abusive conduct.

How long has the conduct been going on, and how regularly.

- Possible evidence of actual foreclosure.

Actual evidence of a market share increase and/or competitors leaving the market

---

[92] Guidance on the Commission's enforcement priorities in applying Article 82 of the EC Treaty to abusive exclusionary conduct by dominant undertakings (2009/C 45/02), [19].
[93] Whish and Bailey, see note 48, at 208.
[94] Commission's Guidance on Art 102, note 92, [20].

- Direct Evidence of any exclusionary strategy.

While the relevance of these factors might be of little relevance to the motor insurance industry by means of abuse of a dominant position may be questionable, their stance as guidelines on what may constitute anti-competitive behaviour is not. Input suppliers being treated favourably or of "particular importance" lies in the same vein as the preferred repair arrangements, the conduct has been happening for a sufficient period of time, and competitors have had to leave the market because of the practice.[95]

In a later paragraph of the Commission' Guidance it is stated that, should the conduct result in consumer harm, there need not be an investigation at all, as anti-competitiveness can be inferred. The example is given that if the undertaking prevents customers from using products of competitors, or provides financial incentives on condition that competitor's products are not tested this would be deemed anti-competitive straight away[96]. The resemblance of this given example and the current happenings in the motor insurance industry is remarkable. Insurance companies, in misleading policyholders by steering them towards an "approved repairer" are doing just this. While the guise of helpfulness and efficiency may be employed, there is a theoretical line that has been crossed.

To give one example FBD insurance provide no information on the fact that consumers are entitled to use their own mechanic after an accident. Instead consumers are lead to believe that attending a FBD Certified Repair Centre is the only option. While the care provided by these certified repair centres is not at all disputed, it is the principle of choice here that is being ignored. Financial incentives of hotel vouchers are offered.[97] This valiant self-promotion, is sound commercial practice but it is effectively deterring policyholders from using their own body shop repairers and closing them off from the market, as well as limiting consumer choice in the process.

---

[95] *Supra* chapter 7(c), "The Irish Market".
[96] Commission's Guidance on Art 102, note 92, [22].
[97] <http://www.fbd.ie/car-insurance/fbd-certified-garages/>.

7.b. Vertical Restraints

Vertical Agreements are made between parties at differing levels of the production process.[98] While some believe them to be harmless to competition, others see that there are dangers posed to the competitive process in allowing them.[99] It is foreseeable that an agreement of this kind could lead to consumer harm, the issue being whether consumers are better off with lower prices and restricted choices or by higher prices and more choices.[100] This strikes the very heart of what is happening in the motor insurance industry. It remains to be seen if insurance steering is beneficial to policyholders in that they have less choice as to where to take their car to be fixed following an altercation, but receive the benefit of a supposedly slightly lowered cost[101] and convenience.

The size of the market in question is a considerable factor. Should the market be small, with few competitors vertical restraints are less likely to have an effect on consumer welfare and choice as there will be a naturally occurring curiosity as to this new product or service, however in a marketplace such as the insurance/bodyshop one there is an abundance of choice and little will on the part of the consumer to venture out into the unknown. Instead there will be more of a willingness to head the advice of a trusted and knowing source (the insurer) and not elect to choose your own repairer, thus diminishing consumer welfare. The Commission has come under criticism for how formally it approaches these restraints. There has been a general feeling that there is a tendency to favour traders and competitors over consumers and their welfare.[102]

There are differing kinds of vertical restraint. While Exclusive Distribution is more focused on territorial concerns, selective distribution is where a supplier chooses to distribute goods only through certain retail outlets, normally because they fit certain criteria regarding expertise. Insurance Steering seems to mimic what this definition provides. Replacing "supplier" for "insurer" and "retail outlet" for "preferred repairer", while considering the act of fixing the damaged car the good, and the similarities are undeniable. There are however conditions to the application of this principle. First, the nature of the product must be assessed. Products benefiting from selective distribution arrangements (SDA) often require

---

[98] Full definition given in Article 1 Regulation 330/2010 [2010] OJ L102/1.

[99] Craig and DeBurca, note 90, page 991.

[100] William Comanor, "Vertical Price-Fixing, Vertical Market Restrictions and the New Antitrust Policy" (1985) 98 Harv L Rev 983, at 1001.

[101] Whether cost levels actually come into the equation is debatable.

[102] Barry Hawk, "System Failure: Vertical Restraints and EC Competition Law", (1995) 32 CML Rev 978.

specialist sales staff, or a particular pitch to maintain a brand image. In *Grohe*[103] it was held that plumbing fittings were not such a specialised product as to warrant a SDA. The obligation upon wholesalers to supply Grohe plumbing fittings only to plumbing contractors was found to be a restriction of competition falling within Article 85 (1), and a restriction of the market.[104] It was also found that the benefits from this SDA were greatly outweighed by the negatives, thus meaning the conditions of Art 81(3) were not fulfilled.[105]

Greater leniency has been awarded to SDAs, as opposed to exclusive distribution agreements as the latter is more likely to cause a divide in the market, something undesirable in the EU's grand plan of a single European market. Other factors with regards SDAs are in need of assessment, such as the possibility of other SDAs in the market having a negative cumulative effect,[106] choice of distribution methods which maximise sales and territorial protection issues. All of this makes it difficult to assess whether an agreement of this nature would be caught by Art 101(1).

In its *Guidelines on Vertical Restraints,*[107] paragraph 110, the Commission suggests four steps be taken in assessing vertical agreements under Art 101 (definition of the relevant market, block exemption application if parties share is below 30 per cent, compatibility with article 101(1) if market share is over 30 per cent, and possible agreement benefits from the exceptions outlined in Art 101(3)). Paragraphs 111 to 121 provide factors relevant to the investigation of agreements under Art 101(1). These include:

- The nature of the agreement

- The market position of the parties

- The market position of competitors

- Entry barriers

- The maturity of the market

- The nature of the product

- The level of trade affected by the agreement

---

[103] Dec 85/44, *Grohe* [1985] OJ L19/17, [1988] 4 CMLR 612.
[104] *Grohe*, at [16].
[105] *Grohe*, at [19]-[20].
[106] Case 75/84 *Metro-SB- Großmärkte GmbH & Co. KG v Commission* (No.2) [1986] ECR 3021.
[107] *Guidelines on Vertical Restraints* OJ [2010] C 130/1.

These may only be some of the listed factors but it is undeniable that when applying these to the practice of insurance steering some red flags do appear. Also included in this list of factors is a potential "cumulative effect" which paragraph 121 describes as being within the market of similar vertical agreements leading to a restriction of competition.

7.c. The Irish Market

In Ireland there have been stirrings that it is time for a clarified stance on the law in this area. From grass roots levels to organisations and people further up the chain, there is a growing recognition that, whether the practice of insurance steering is anti-competitive or not, there is a need for a constant right to freedom of choice on the part of consumers. This market is one facing a subtle imbalance of power, however within its subtlety lies a potential deadly threat.

In Northern Ireland an active campaign has been taken to highlight the issue. The Northern Ireland Bodyshop Alliance (NIBA) has claimed that thousands of drivers are being misled by insurance companies, and that they are unaware that they have the freedom to attend a bodyshop of their choosing. The NIBA movement has grown to such a level that a campaign of "Your Car, Your Choice" has been launched.[108] Genuine fears have arose that restricting consumer choice has the effect of distorting the market, but may also lead to a loss of local jobs.[109] Further concerns have been raised that Insurance companies are increasing pressure on repairers to do cheaper work, cut corners and even compromise safety standards in some cases. There has been call in Northern Ireland for Stormont to intervene and guarantee a transparent commercial environment.[110]

In Ireland a similar movement is beginning to emerge. Although operating on a smaller scale to NIBA the Vehicle Repairers Association (VRA) has begun a similar campaign in Ireland. The organisation seeks to address the increasing pressures on work volumes and margins bodyshops face, as well as the need for training and investment. Ultimately the objective is to

---

[108] "NI Car Repairers Warn Over Motorist Safety" <http://www.niba.biz/niba-trade-news/144-ni-car-repairers-warn-over-motorist-safety.html> (visited 2 January 2015).
[109] Sean Bradley, Chairman of NIBA, "NI bodyshops warn of local jobs threat" <http://www.autobiz.ie/news/ni-bodyshops-warn-of-local-jobs-threat.html> (visited 2 January 2015).
[110] "NIBA warns Insurance Tactics could Compromise Safety", <http://www.autobiz.ie/news/niba-warns-insurance-tactics-could-compromise-safety.html> (visited 2 January 2015).

have repairer's rights adequately represented, as it is an industry that has been very fragmented in the past.[111]

When it was starting out, the VRA issued questionnaires to prospective members, asking them, amongst other matters, to outline anything that they felt was having an adverse effect on their business.[112] Many of them stated their top concern was Insurance Companies pushing people into using their network of approved repairers. A bodyshop in Cork stated the "undue influence" of the insurance companies meant they could dictate terms and rates. Another in Dublin deemed the insurance companies behaviour as "aggressive" in steering customers. A bodyshop in Cavan referred to the "stranglehold" insurance companies had on the supply of work. Multiple repairers used the terminology of "forcing" customers, while one in Dublin went as far to call it "bullying". All of this points clearly towards dissatisfaction and frustration in the industry. An issue effecting so many small businesses in Ireland and causing such distortion and a sense of unfairness in the market demands to be properly addressed.

It is not just internal to the industry that these concerns have been raised. Consumer Expert Tina Leonard has spoken out about the pressure consumers are facing from their insurance company to use a particular garage for repairs, how they are offered incentives to do so and led to believe they do not have a choice in the matter. It was emphasised that the right to choose is one of the utmost importance, going to the core of consumer rights, and that, if one so wishes, they may use a local repairer. Concerns were also echoed that the constant cost reductions in relation to insurance work were damaging and that this could lead to potential quality and safety issues[113].

The main benefit insurance companies cite in support of a network of approved repairers is a reduction in the hourly labour rate. Approved bodyshops offer lower rates in the hope of increased repair volume, this in turn causes a bidding war between bodyshops and downward pressure on repairer costs in 2007 the average hourly rate was €52 per hour for insurance work, in 2014 this dropped to €35 per hour.[114] When this is compared to an €85 euro an hour charge for oil changing and basic mechanical servicing by a main car dealership, it is highly worrying. When dealing with referrals from insurer, the repairer is making the car road-worthy again. It is logical that the charge for this should be higher than running routine

---

[111] <http://www.vra.ie/index_files/Page329.htm> (visited 2 January 2015).
[112] The following sources have remained confidential and anonymous.
[113] "Pat Kenny RTE show highlights "Your Car Your Choice" concept"
<http://www.vra.ie/index_files/Page332.htm> (visited 2 January 2015).
[114] From research conducted by the VRA in 2014.

checks and less complicated jobs. Concerns of this type have arisen in Australia[115], where it is feared that cutting costs may have adverse effects on the quality of repairs.

There has been apprehension also as to whether these claims of price benefits actually hold true at all. In speaking to NIBA in 2011, insurance industry executive Martin McRandall gave a breakdown of insurance companies financial figures. Based on his calculations, on average, 70% of claims pay-outs were for personal injury claims, 15% for the insured's vehicle damage and 13% on third party damage. It was also estimated that two thirds of claims related to vehicles that were repaired and one third on write-offs. Further to this it was estimated that out of gross premiums paid on motor vehicles, only 7.5% actually went towards the cost of vehicle repair. This begs the question, where does the other 92.5% go? And why are insurance companies relying so insistently on the benefit of cost reductions a network of approved repairers provides when it is obviously not a pressing concern of theirs, cost-wise?

It is worth noting that a system of recommended repairers may work in densely populated areas, but in rural areas, the negative effects of this practice are magnified. Approved repairers rely on a certain volume of work to remain profitable. Meanwhile vehicle population in certain parts of Ireland remains small, at least not large enough to support the volume of work an approved repairer would require to remain afloat. As a result many Irish counties find themselves having to travel long distances to get to one of these insurer certified repairers, simply because they were under the impression they were obligated to do so.

Many autobody repairers around the country have lost work because of this practice of steering. Insurers have been said to look for purchase invoices before payment was made, steer customers away from repairers after the repairer assessed and quoted damages, and insinuate a non-approved repairer is not good enough to complete to job at hand.[116] Many repairers have expressed great frustration over these practices. One spoke of a customer who wanted to have her car repaired with the local repairer of her choosing, but was steered towards an AXA certified garage as the excess she would have to pay would be €100, as opposed to €300 her local repairer was offering. While the local bodyshop attempted to absorb some of this excess themselves, competing with such a ludicrously low quote was near impossible for them. The consumer was left with no option but to go with the insurer's suggestion. Another sole trader in the auto bodyshop industry said he has seen a 60%

---

[115] "Cutting Costs Leading to Cutting Corners in Australian Bodyshop Sector"
<http://www.autobiz.ie/news/cutting-costs-leading-to-cutting-corners-in-australian-bodyshop-sector.html#sthash.6CpjKWSo.dpuf>.
[116] Taken from email correspondence with various auto body-shops around Ireland, January 2015.

reduction in business since 2008. While the economic downturn at this time was a factor, the other main contributing factor was due to people being "uncomfortable defying their insurance companies" and being "bullied" into a choice they did not want to make. Through correspondence with these autobody repairers, a few have spoken of unethical practices on the part of those involved in this network of approved repairers. Golfing trips and gifts have been offered by repairers already in the network to insurance executives in order to receive more business and keep on the insurance companies "good side". While in theory there is nothing wrong with this practice, it does demonstrate that there is a need for a more transparent legal environment. The general feeling amongst many in the industry is that this practice is undercutting business to such a level that it is very difficult to compete at all, and due to this consumers are not having their choices listened too.

The issue has even reached the political sphere. In 2011 TD Robert Dowds put it to the Minister that this anti-competitive issue was not in the public's best interest.[117] He stated that insurance companies were purposely slower in processing claims for consumers who chose not to use one of their approved repairers. He noted that he had received reports of insurance companies who insisted a claimant use a repairer a great distance away, when there are local repairers who would do the same job for a similar price. Attention was drawn to the fact that similar practices are happening in other areas, such as with house insurance and windscreen repairs, and how it has subsequently been condemned in these areas. Dowds called for change in the industry in order to help small businesses remain afloat and keep the value of consumer choice intact.[118]

8. The American Stance

The American jurisdiction is the one which has addressed the issue of insurance steering best. Particularly in recent years a considerable amount of case law ruling that the practice is anti-competitive has emerged. 35 American States have some form of legislation addressing insurance steering.[119] All of these various laws from various states say a similar thing- no

---

[117] Dowds Speech, note 52.
[118] Email correspondence with Dowds further to this speech was unsuccessful.
[119] <http://www.stopdrp.com/steering-laws-by-state.html> (visited 23 October 2014).

insurer can suggest or recommend that an automobile be repaired at a specific automotive repair dealer.[120]

The law on anti-trusts and anti-competitive behaviour stems from the Sherman Act, the first measure passed by the U.S Congress outlawing trusts.[121] The basic purpose of this Act was intended to be threefold: to outlaw any contracts in restraint of trade, any combinations in restraint of trade and conspiracies in restraint of trade.[122] While problems regarding interpretation of this may have been an issue, the rationale behind it has remained largely unchanged over the years.[123]

The most prominent case emerging in recent years has been that of *Artie's Auto Body, Inc. et al. v. The Hartford Fire Insurance Company*[124] in which the Connecticut Auto Repair Shop Owners Association won a 10 year legal battle. It was alleged that the defendant was engaged in unfair and deceptive acts and practices by steering customers who had suffered an altercation to certain preferred repair shops. The Court applied Connecticut's own established three-pronged "cigarette rule" used for determining unfair trade practices. The criteria for this being that the practice offends public policy, is immoral, unethical, oppressive or unscrupulous or causes substantial injury to consumers, competitors or other business persons. For a practice to satisfy this test it need only fulfil one of these.[125] In this case it was found that the first principle of public policy was the main issue here, as the defendant's acts came within the "penumbra"[126] of some common law, regulatory, or statutory or other established concept of unfairness. As long as this can be demonstrated, the plaintiff need not show of any literal violation. Jennings J upheld the 2009 decision and the award of $14.77 million in damages and added a further $20 million in punitive damages.[127] In his concluding paragraphs Jennings noted that there is much pressure and influence in this area, where "service standards are much more than suggestions" but more an "obvious and conscious

---

[120] California Insurance Code Section 758.5 (b)(1).
[121] <http://www.infoplease.com/encyclopedia/history/sherman-antitrust-act.html> (visited 3 January 2015).
[122] The Sherman Act (1890) Section 1.
[123] William Letwin, *Law and Economic Policy in America: The Evolution of the Sherman Anti-Trust Act* (University of Chicago Press, 1981) at 144.
[124] *Artie's Auto Body, Inc. et al. v. The Hartford Fire Insurance Company* (2013) Connecticut Superior Court, Docket No: X08-CV03-0196141S.
[125] *Harris v. Memorial Hospital and Health Center*, (2010) 296 Conn. 315, 350.
[126] "Penumbra" being defined as "a vague, indefinite, or borderline area" in footnote 2 of the *Hartford* case.
[127] "US Insurer Hit with Massive "Steering" Fine",
<http://www.autobiz.ie/news/US_Insurer_Hit_With_Massive_ldquosteeringrdquo_Fine.html> (visited 6 October 2014).

effort to influence". It was later noted that the punitive damages awarded were to serve as a deterrent to other insurance carriers, warning them off engaging in similar unlawful conduct.[128]

In the state of New York, It was not until only a few years ago that the regard towards insurance steering shifted. In 2011 *North State Autobahn Inc. v Progressive Insurance Group*[129] upheld the previous precedence in that the plaintiff could not show a broad enough impact on consumers, that there was no real evidence of actual harm or deceptive or misleading behaviour on the insurers part and also that even if harm had been caused to consumers, harm to the plaintiff would only be derivative of this and not actionable by the plaintiff.[130]

However a year later upon appeal the decision was overturned.[131] It was recognised that "[P]arties claiming the benefit of [General Business Law § 349(h)] must, at the threshold, charge conduct that is consumer oriented".[132] The appellate court found that the complainant had in fact sufficiently demonstrated that there had been a "broad impact on consumers at large".[133] It was said that any action taken by a business competitor protecting their own interest will ultimately serve to protect the interests of the consuming public.[134]

In a Louisiana case it was even stated that insurer's repair facilities were pressurised into forgoing certain repairs to vehicle that any other prudent repairer would deem necessary.[135] This action was taken on the part of the public interest, with the Attorney General calling it a "national problem".[136] The Attorney General of Connecticut has also called for the

---

[128] Paraphrased from David Slossberg's quote in "The Hartford hit with $20 million in damages", <http://www.hssklaw.com/News-Events/The-Hartford-hit-with-20-million-in-damages.shtml> (visited 26 October 2014).

[129] *North State Autobahn Inc. v Progressive Insurance Group* (2010) 2761/07 Supreme Court of Westchester County.

[130] New York, General Business Law, NY Code, No. 349.

[131] *North State Autobahn, Inc. v Progressive Ins. Group Co.* (2012) NY Slip Op 06932.

[132] *New York Univ. v Continental Ins. Co.*, (1995) 87 NY2d 308, at 320.

[133] *Oswego Laborers' Local 214 Pension Fund v Marine Midland Bank*, (1995) 85 NY2d, at 25.

[134] "NY Appellate Court Issues 'Monumental' Steering Decision" (2012). <http://collision.honda.com/ny-appellate-court-issues-monumental-steering-decision#.VJBuiivF9qM> (visited 26 October 2014).

[135] *State of Louisiana, James D. "Buddy" Caldwell, Attorney General v State Farm ... Mutual Automobile Insurance Co.* (2012) Div. 432829, Docket No. SEC26, at [32].

[136] James M. Burns, "Louisiana Attorney General Files Suit Against State Farm Alleging Monopolization and "Deceptive Trade Practices"", <http://www.dickinson-wright.com/news-alerts/insurance-antitrust-legal-news-volume-3-number-5?utm_source=Mondaq&utm_medium=syndication&utm_campaign=View-Original> (visited 27 October 2014).

enforcement of "anti-steering" laws to be a nationwide priority.[137] The National Conference of Insurance Legislators (NCOIL) has even recommended a model bill encouraging states to include anti-steering language in insurance regulations,[138] section 6.B of which proposes that insurers should not make recommendations to policyholders unless expressly asked to do so.

While the stance on Insurance Steering Laws appears to be positive by many there are others who are not so pleased with the developments in this area, claiming these laws have the potential to damage the business of the insurance companies. They claim that recommendation networks and the better consumer service flowing from it represent the free market at its best, that removing the ability of insurance companies to steer a customer in a certain direction violates their right to commercial speech.[139] There seems to be a misunderstanding here as to what the objective of anti-steering legislation is intended for. Anti-steering law have been incorrectly interpreted as a blanket ban on a class of speech, and a ruse under the "easily misused" guise of consumer protection.[140] The value of free speech is not what is at question here. Recommendations are still available at the request of the consumer. Anti-steering laws do not have the effect of limiting the information provided to consumers but instead enhances it, allowing them to have their own free choice. The insurer's right to free commercial speech remains wholly intact and consumers rights are not compromised in the process. It is recognised that these networks have their benefits and many consumers have no issue with being given a helpful recommendation by their insurer, however a line is crossed when the insurer misleads the consumer into believing their own solution is the only option available. This is what anti-steering legislation is targeted at. The majority of this opposition is coming from insurance companies in some form, however their arguments are unfounded. Citing the long line of case law regarding commercial speech does not change the fact that it is essentially irrelevant to what anti-steering legislation hopes to

---

[137] Connecticut Attorney General, Press Release from 1st September 2009
<http://www.ct.gov/ag/cwp/view.asp?A=2341&Q=446066> (visited 27 October 2014).
[138] "National Conference of Insurance Legislators, Proposed Model Act Regarding Motor Vehicle Crash Parts and Repair" <http://www.ncoil.org/docs/aftermarketmodel.pdf>.
[139] The value of Commercial Speech was noted by the Supreme Court in *Central Hudson Gas & Electric Corp. v. Public Service Commission* 447 U.S. 557, 561 (1980).
[140] Orrin Harrison and J.Carl Cecere Jr. "'Anti-Steering' Insurance Laws: State Censorship of Consumer Information Treads on First Amendment Rights" (2010), 25 Washington Legal Foundation 6, at 3.

achieve.[141] Instead it is a thinly veiled attempt by insurers and those representing them to cast doubt over something which is desperately needed in order to regulate a one-sided industry.

Another argument put forward against anti-steering law is that it is actually insulting to consumers, implying that they are "too spineless" to insist that they want their own body-shop worker to do the job, or "too stupid" to do any independent evaluation of information of their own.[142] While the terminology of this argument may be unnecessarily harsh, the core value of it is true, yet instead of it being a lack of intelligence it is rather a lack of information, and where to find this information. Having to make a claim with an insurance company is not something people have to do on a regular basis, therefore it is understandable that there would be a lack of knowledge on their part as to what their specific rights are. If consumers are not made aware at the very first hurdle (i.e. putting a call into their insurer) that they do in fact have a choice, they are unlikely to seek out this information at a later stage, and if they do, it would be too late. Insurance companies are, after all, businesses. They have a product to sell and want to employ the most persuasive mechanisms available to them to sell. It is only natural that consumer would be drawn to this and influenced, but the fact remains that the choice to choose otherwise remains open and available to them, so as to make an informed decision. Protecting consumers from making potentially bad choices is not a justification for giving them no choice at all.

9. Conclusion

The practice of insurance steering is one which needs to be assessed from the viewpoint of the insurer, the repairer, and the consumer. This, teamed with an assessment of Irish law, current Irish standing, evaluation of the possible breaches it imposes, as well as analysis of European law and the American jurisdiction points toward the fact that the law in the area desperately needs clarification. From the Competition's Guidance Note on the issue it is apparent there is a lack of understanding as to what the actual conditions are in the market in reality. European Law demonstrates that there are a fair amount of potential grounds for a claim of breach to be based and through American precedence it has transpired that stopping this possibly damaging practice can have its advantages. Whatever the future of this area may

---

[141] See "Restricting in Auto Repair Hurts Consumers", a joint paper by the American Insurance Association, National Association of Mutual Insurance Companies and Property Casualty Insurers Association of America <http://www.pciaa.net/web/sitehome.nsf/lcpublic/419/$file/amp-industry_one_pager.pdf>.
[142] Harrison and Cecere, note 140, at 4.

be it is the consumer who will find themselves with the largest loss or gain. Their interests and welfare are what needs protecting from anti-competitive practices. If this practice is not stopped and/or clarified in the motor trade industry the practice may become more prominent in other areas, already insurance companies have started dictating which plumbers and builders homeowners should use. If some kind of action is not taken soon, matters in this area will only deteriorate further, the barriers to entry in the market will heighten and the power insurance companies hold only become stronger. The imbalances here need to be addressed, otherwise the problem will only worsen and remain overlooked, as they have been done for too long.

10. Bibliography

I.   Table of Legislation

Irish- Acts

Central Bank Act 1989

Competition Act 2002

Competition and Consumer Protection Act 2014

Consumer Act 2007

Consumer Protection Code 2012

Insurance Act 1936

Insurance Act 1995

Insurance Act 1989

Insurance Act 2000

Irish- Other

Non-Life Insurance (Provision of Information) (Renewal of Policy of Insurance) Regulations (2007), S.I. No. 74/2007.

The Competition Authority, Competition Issues in the Non-Life Insurance Market (March 2005).

Competition Authority Guidance Note: Preferred Repairer Arrangements in the Insurance Sector (December 2012).

Europe

Commission Guidelines on the Application of Article 81(3) [2004] OJ C101/97

Commission Guidelines I the Application of Article [101(3)] of the Treaty Guidelines OJ [2004] C 130/1

European Commission, XV Annual Report on Competition Policy 1985 (1986).

European Communities (Non-Life Insurance) Framework Regulations 1994   Council Regulation 1/2003 of 16 December 2002 on the Implementation of the Rules on Competition laid down in Articles 81 and 82 of the Treaty [2003] OJ L1/1.

EC Commission, "Guidelines on the method of Setting Fines" pursuant to Article 23(2)(a) of Regulation No 1/2003 [2006] OJ C210/2

Guidance on the Commission's enforcement priorities in applying Article 82 of the EC Treaty to abusive exclusionary conduct by dominant undertakings (2009/C 45/02)

Guidelines on Vertical Restraints OJ [2010] C 130/1

Memo of the European Commission, Antitrust: Commission welcomes General Court Judgment Upholding its Decision Against Intel (2014) MEMO/14/416

Regulation 330/2010 [2010] OJ L102/1

Treaty for the Functioning of the European Union

America

California Insurance Code Section 758.5 (b)(1)

New York, General Business Law, NY Code, No. 349

The Sherman Act (1890)

Wisconsin State Legislature, Chapter 632 Subchapter IV, Automobile and Motor Vehicle Insurance

II. Table of Cases

Abbot v Howard (1832) Hayes 381

Artie's Auto Body, Inc et al v The Hartford Fire Insurance Company (2013) Connecticut Superior Court, Docket No: X08-CV03-0196141S

C-435/99 *Courage Ltd v Crehan* [1999] ECR I-6297

Case C-234/89 *Delimitis v Henninger Brau AG* [1991] ECR I-935

Case C-41/90 *Hofner and Elser v Macroton GmbH* [1991] ECR I-1979

Case 56/65 *Societe La Technique Minere v Maschinenbau Ulm GmbH* [1996] ECR 235

Case C-8/08 *T-Mobile Netherlands* [2009] ECR I-4529

Case 75/84 *Metro-SB- Großmärkte GmbH & Co. KG v Commission (No.2)* [1986] ECR 3021.

Cases T- 374/94 *European Night Services v Commission* [1998] ECR II-3141, [1998] 5 CMLR 718

Case T 112/99 *Metropole Television (M6) Suez-Lyonnaise des Eaux, France Telecom, and Television Francaise 1 SA (TFI) v Commission* [2001] ECR II-2459

Central Hudson Gas & Electric Corp. v. Public Service Commission (1980) 447 U.S. 557, 561

Crehan v Inntrepreneur CPC [2003] EWHC 1510; [2004] EWCa Civ 637

Dec No 274, *Falcon Holidays/Ben McArdle Ltd*, 4 Feb 1994 and Notif CA/31/92E.

Dec 85/44, *Grohe* [1985] OJ L19/17, [1988] 4 CMLR 612

Dec No 1, *Nallen/O'Toole* 2 April 1992, Notif CA/8/91.

Établissements Consten S.à.R.L. and Grundig-Verkaufs-GmbH v Commission of the European Economic Community (56/64, 58/64) [1966] ECR 299

GlaxoSmithKline v Commission

GlaxoSmithKline Services Unlimited v Commission of the EC (T-168/01) [2006] E.C.R. II-2969; (C-501/06 P, C-513/06 P, C-515/06 P, C-519/06 P) [2009] 4 C.M.L.R. 2

Harris v. Memorial Hospital and Health Center, (2010) 296 Conn. 315

Inspector Murphy v PMPA Insurance Company [1978] ILRM 29.

National Society of Professional Engineers v US (1978), 435, US 679

North State Autobahn Inc. v Progressive Insurance Group (2010) 2761/07 Supreme Court of Westchester County; (2012) NY Slip Op 06932

New York Univ. v Continental Ins. Co. (1995) 87 NY2d 308

Oswego Laborers' Local 214 Pension Fund v Marine Midland Bank (1995) 85 NY2d, at 25

Phillip M. Proctor v State Farm Mutual Automobile Insurance Company 675 F.2d 308 (D.C. Cir. 1982)

Quality Auto Body Inc v Allstate Insurance Company 660 F2d 1195 (1981)

Standard Oil v US 221 US (1911)

State of Louisiana, James D. "Buddy" Caldwell, Attorney General v State Farm ... Mutual Automobile Insurance Co. (2012) Div. 432829, Docket No. SEC26

Shinedean Ltd. v Alldown Demolition (London) Ltd. [2006] EWCA Civ 939

III. Books

Breuel, Brian H., *The Complete Idiots Guide to Buying Insurance and Annuities* (Alpha, 1996).

Brue, Stanley and McConnell, Campbell, and Flynn, Sean, *Essentials of Economics* (3rd ed., McGraw Hill Irwin, 2014).

Craig, Paul and DeBurca, Grainne, *European Law: Text, Cases and Materials* (5th ed., Oxford University Press, 2011)

Letwin, William, *Law and Economic Policy in America: The Evolution of the Sherman Anti-Trust Act* (University of Chicago Press, 1981)

Lowry, John, and Rawlings, Philip and Merkin, Robert, *Insurance Law: Doctrines and Principles* (3rd ed., Hart Publishing, 2011)

McCarthy, Alan WJ and Power, Vincent, *Irish Competition Law: The Competition Act 2002* (Tottel, 2006)

O'Regan Cazabon, Attracta, *Insurance Law in Ireland* (Round Hall Sweet and Maxwell, 1999)

Pierse, Robert, *Road Traffic Law* (2nd ed., Butterworths, 1995)

Power, Vincent, Competition Law and Practice (Tottel, 2007)

Scherer, Fredric and Ross, David, *Industrial Market Structure and Economic Performance* (3rd ed., Houghton Mifflin, 1990)

Weatherill, Stephen, *EU Consumer Law and Policy* (Edward Elgar, 2005)

Whish, Richard and Bailey, David, *Competition Law* (7th ed., Oxford University Press, 2012)

IV. Articles

Comanor, William, "Vertical Price-Fixing, Vertical Market Restrictions and the New Antitrust Policy" (1985) 98 Harv L Rev 983

Harrison, Orrin and Cecere J.Carl Jr. "'Anti-Steering' Insurance Laws: State Censorship of Consumer Information Treads on First Amendment Rights" (2010), 25 Washington Legal Foundation 6

Hawk, Barry, "System Failure: Vertical Restraints and EC Competition Law", (1995) 32 CML Rev 978

Jedličková, Barbora, "One among many or one above all? The role of consumers and their welfare in competition law and policy" (2012), 33(12) ECLR 574.

Korah, Valentine "The Rise and Fall of Provisional Validity – The Need for a Rule of Reason in EEC Anti-trust" (1981) 3 North Western Journal of International Business Law, 320

Maher, Imelda, "A Fine Balance, The National Courts, The European Commission and EU Competition Law" (2011) 1 DULJ 153.

Nebel, Rolf, "Application of Competition Law in the Insurance Industry" [1993] 5 ECLR 189.

Odudu, Okeoghene, "Interpreting Article 81(1): Object as Subjective Intention (2001) 26 EL Rev 60

Tormey, Shelia, "Legislative Comment- Ireland: the Competition and Consumer Protection Act 2014" (2014) 35(11) ECLR 534.

Whish Richard, and Surfin, Brenda "Article 85 and the Rule of Reason" (1987) 7 YBEL 12-20

V. Websites

<http://www.ccpc.ie/who-we-are>

<http://www.centralbank.ie/regulation/industry-sectors/insurance-companies/non-life-insurance-companies/Pages/default.aspx>

<http://www.claim.ie/Road_Accident>

<http://www.consumerhelp.ie/making-a-claim>

<http://www.fbd.ie/car-insurance/fbd-certified-garages/>

<http://www.infoplease.com/encyclopedia/history/sherman-antitrust-act.html>

<http://www.stopdrp.com/steering-laws-by-state.html> (visited October 2nd 2014).

<http://www.vra.ie/index_files/Page329.htm>

VI. Web Articles

"Louisiana Attorney General Files Suit Against State Farm Alleging Monopolization and "Deceptive Trade Practices"", <http://www.dickinson-wright.com/news-alerts/insurance-antitrust-legal-news-volume-3-number--5?utm_source=Mondaq&utm_medium=syndication&utm_campaign=View-Original>

"NI bodyshops warn of local jobs threat" <http://www.autobiz.ie/news/ni-bodyshops-warn-of-local-jobs-threat.html>

"NI Car Repairers Warn Over Motorist Safety" <http://www.niba.biz/niba-trade-news/144-ni-car-repairers-warn-over-motorist-safety.html>

"NIBA warns Insurance Tactics could Compromise Safety", <http://www.autobiz.ie/news/niba-warns-insurance-tactics-could-compromise-safety.html>

"NY Appellate Court Issues 'Monumental' Steering Decision" (2012) <http://collision.honda.com/ny-appellate-court-issues-monumental-steering-decision#.VJBuiivF9qM>

"Pat Kenny RTE show highlights "Your Car Your Choice" concept" <http://www.vra.ie/index_files/Page332.htm>

"The Hartford hit with $20 million in damages", <http://www.hssklaw.com/News-Events/The-Hartford-hit-with-20-million-in-damages.shtml>

"US Insurer Hit with Massive "Steering" Fine" <http://www.autobiz.ie/news/US_Insurer_Hit_With_Massive_ldquosteeringrdquo_Fine.html>

VII. Miscellaneous

Competition Commission, "Empowering and Protecting Consumers: Consultation on Institutional Changes for Provision of Consumer Information, Education, Advocacy, and Enforcement: Competition Commission Response" (September 2011)

Connecticut Attorney General, Press Release from 1st September 2009 <http://www.ct.gov/ag/cwp/view.asp?A=2341&Q=446066>

Dillon Eustace, A Guide to Non-Life Regulation in Ireland (February 2011) <http://hb.betterregulation.com/external/A%20Guide%20to%20Non-Life%20Insurance%20Regulation%20in%20Ireland.pdf>

"National Conference of Insurance Legislators, Proposed Model Act Regarding Motor Vehicle Crash Parts and Repair" <http://www.ncoil.org/docs/aftermarketmodel.pdf>

OFT, "A Competition Regime for Growth: A Consultation on Options for Reform, The OFT's Response to the Government's Consultation" (June 2011) (OFT, Competition Consultation)

"Restricting in Auto Repair Hurts Consumers", a joint paper by the American Insurance Association, National Association of Mutual Insurance Companies and Property Casualty Insurers Association of America <http://www.pciaa.net/web/sitehome.nsf/lcpublic/419/$file/amp-industry_one_pager.pdf>

Robert Dowds Speech, "Government Action is needed to End Insurance Company 'Steering'" (November 2011)

VIII. Primary Sources

Email correspondence with auto bodyshop repairers (who preferred to remain anonymous) 2015

VRA questionnaires 2014